S0-DUH-175

Dear Laura,

"Some day you must walk in
The woods – alone and close
to God".  Page 40

Affectionately

James W Dwyer

# Dreams of Destiny

"Our destiny offers, not the cup of despair, but the chalice of opportunity. So let us seize it, not in fear, but in gladness—and 'riders on the earth together,' let us go forward, firm in our faith, steadfast in our purpose, cautious of the dangers; but sustained by our confidence in the will of God and the promise of man."

Richard Milhous Nixon
*President of the United States*

II

# Dreams of Destiny

By

James F. O'Dwyer

Publishers

willow house
Stockton, California

Copyright © 1970 by James F. O'Dwyer

Library of Congress Catalog Card No. 70-103978
Printed in the United States of America

Dedicated

To

CHARLES CHRISTOPHER CRESPI

Photographs
Inspired and Produced

by


Kenichi Nakata

# Acknowledgments

In various ways many people have assisted me in the preparation of this text. It is my good fortune to have the opportunity of meeting several people every day who reveal to me new horizons yet to be reached and new peaks yet to be conquered. For this reason I am indebted to every person that I have ever known. Where the indebtedness is so extensive it is difficult to be specific.

I owe a special debt of gratitude to Mrs. Andrew Cademartori for her wonderful skill in deciphering the original manuscript.

I salute the Stockton City Police Department and the staff at the Sheriff's Office of San Joaquin County, California, for their kind cooperation.

I am mindful, too, of you who read these pages. I do not petition pardon for all that I have left unsaid. To do otherwise would be singularly presumptuous on my part because others have more to say and the charisma to say it better. Neither will I seek to engage your gratitude if what I have to say stimulates a new dimension of love and trust in your daily life. We all share in the blessing which one of us achieves. The dream is that the reader will discover the startling vistas of the dawn and share the discovery with others. Towards the fulfillment of that dream this work is respectfully presented to the people.

James F. O'Dwyer

STOCKTON, (Advent 1969)

# Contents

# Preface

There are many talented and concerned observers of human conduct today and individually they represent a great many different social disciplines. They mostly tend to be concerned with tomorrow and record today's events as to what the effect will be at a future time. These reporters are not necessarily right simply because they have recorded their observations, which in a great many cases are merely opinions based on their personal feelings.

They do however, serve an extremely valuable purpose in that their views, along with many others, receive some exposure to those elements of our society who will take the time to receive opinions other than their own. As described in this book, man's destiny for tomorrow is based on his beliefs and acts of today. The day after tomorrow is not the time for fighting dragons, it is the time for being.

Any discussion of child-parent relationships, authority, discipline, control, love, hate, costumes, dirt, eroticism, or learning any lesson without experience, provides an example that concerns this generation and change.

Change itself is not the concern. What is important is the basis for change, the pattern of change, and the relationship of change to time. For several years change used to be developed over long periods, but now it is instantaneous and immediate. Frequently, it takes place before its previous difference is even completed. We are different because of change, as for instance, today we discuss love as a cause not as a result.

The author of this work seeks to combine the many changes of society with our sound morality so that our lives will be more fully understood.

There is great need today to express such points of view so that they may be used as building blocks for a foundation on which we all may then survive the flood of an affluent materialistic society.

Michael N. Canlis, Sheriff-Corner
San Joaquin County, California

· PADRE ·
JVNIPERO ·
SERRA ·
FOVNDER ·
OF · THE ·
CALIFORNIA ·
MISSIONS ·
· 1713 – 1784 ·

# The Dream

The men who came to California before and during the Gold Rush have been loosely called pioneers of the Wild West. Some were derelict denizens of saloon bars, these built nothing, they left nothing to posterity. Others were brave and left an enduring mark on the continent which they fashioned. These were real pioneers.

A pioneer is one who goes before to clear the way for others. He may be one who risks his life blazing a new trail, opening up new territories or launching into the stratosphere to land on the moon, or taking his stand on the high pinnacles of vision above the milling prosaic crowd. But whatever his vision or work or endeavor, he is essentially one who rises above the surging mass of people and goes up on to the high places where he can enter into communion with the things above.

A pioneer is a leader, one who steps out before others. He, who falls back to listen and imbibe the patter of the crowd, ceases to be a pioneer. The slow poison of mediocrity seeps through him, and he is in danger of being drugged to the insensibility of the mediocre. A pioneer must have vision and courage —that vision of our fathers that we should live "in the land of the free and the home of the brave."

That was the dream of our ancestors. They proclaimed the fundamental rights of man, his magnificent dignity, his individual identity, and his exalted destiny. They acknowledged that all human life is sacred and that it deserves our unmitigated respect. On this simple principle our forefathers based their dreams of destiny.

Destiny may be defined as the sequence of events after death which is shaped and determined by current conduct. It involves an understanding that responsibility is the ability to respond to the needs and rights of others. This surely necessitates an awareness of the problems that confront people and a willingness to stem the tides of loneliness, discrimination and the fear of the unknown and uncertain future. This attitude is not unconstructive or uncreative. It does not prevent problems by force and fear, but by drawing forth a tremendous response of love and trust in the two great natures — the human and the divine.

The destiny of any man is shaped by his own evaluation of life, love and the search for truth. No man possesses the fullness of these because every man is born to seek perfection by trial and error, by experimentation and education, and most of all by contemplating his destiny which is discovered at the moment of death. We are born not only to live and love, but also to die and live again. The dream of man's final destiny is inspired by the words of Quoheleth as they are recorded in the third chapter of Ecclesiastes:

There is a season for everything, a time for every occupation under heaven:

2

*A time for giving birth,*
*a time for dying;*
*a time for planting,*
*a time for uprooting what has been planted.*

*A time for killing,*
*a time for healing;*
*a time for knocking down,*
*a time for building.*

*A time for tears,*
*a time for laughter;*
*a time for mourning,*
*a time for dancing.*

*A time for throwing stones away,*
*a time for gathering them up;*
*a time for embracing,*
*a time to refrain from embracing.*

*A time for searching,*
*a time for losing;*
*a time for keeping,*
*a time for throwing away.*

*A time for tearing,*
*a time for sewing;*
*a time for keeping silent,*
*a time for speaking.*

*A time for loving,*
*a time for hating;*
*a time for war,*
*a time for peace.*

These words inspire an honest examination of conscience in preparation for the inevitable and inexorable destiny. National laws and State statutes may assist us to achieve the destiny but in the last analysis these factors must be backed by vigorous public opinion springing from a true concept of the nobility of the immortal soul of each individual.

This is an age of propagandists in which the people are daily saturated by slogans and cliches. Too often our thinking is done for us in tabloid form. It is not the thinking-people with high ideals that dominate the world. It is the "average-man" with his aphorisms culled from superficial movies and novels and yellow press pandering to the crowd that flaunts himself on the scene.

What fifty thousand say may be right but it does not become right merely because a large crowd says it. "Vox populi, vox Dei" —the voice of the people is the voice of God—is true only when the voice of the people is proclaiming what is the genuine hallmarked law of God. The cliches of crowds or individuals prove nothing. Like the scarlet figure of history we dare not wash our hands of our responsibilities and so become Pontius Pilates of the twentieth century. The weakness of human nature must not be allowed to brutalize men and women or defraud their children by taking the bloom of youth from the fair forehead of love and leaving the home nothing more than the gaunt embers of a wonderful dream.

To dream of destiny is not only beautiful, it is also brave. The achievement of that dream will lift our nation to a brilliant place in the sun. Fighting dragons may be the heroic fanciful saga of the middle ages, but in another sense we are all living the epic life now. "Your duty," wrot Dag Hammarskjold, "your reward, your destiny is in the present moment."

# Signs of Sadness

All over the world, from Berlin to Brazil, from Chile to China, people of all milieus and cultures are frantically aware of the frenzied confusion and chaos that have engulfed this planet. Throughout the world one thousand people commit suicide every day. In Japan someone kills himself every thirty minutes.

In 1967 six million students enrolled in American universities, but within two months more than seventy demonstrations enveloped our campuses. Almost five million of our teenagers now suffer emotional disturbances. Each year approximately three hundred thousand single girls have abortions in the United States. It is estimated that 50% of all teen-marriages end in divorce within five years. A recent UNESCO survey indicates that 60% of European and American women are frustrated and unhappy. The Senate Armed Service Committee has reported (March 6, 1969) that a total of 150,536 soldiers, sailors, marines, and air force men were absent-without-leave between mid 1967 and mid 1968. These figures indicate a defection in the Armed Service almost every three minutes.

The graph of suicide, divorce, illegitimacy, venereal disease, and shop lifting has attained a peak that was unknown in the apogee of the Babylonian or Roman Empires.

Many people will tell you that our youth are a menace to society, but that is true only to the extent that society first menaced them. Teenagers in the United States represent 9% of our total population. The real menace that lurks in the path of life is the loss of respect for morality and legitimate authority.

Fifty years ago when my father was a boy he was taught to obey those in authority. I do not claim that people are less willing to obey today than in former times. In fact there are more people obeying others in the world now than ever before. But obedience has changed its direction. Our fathers obeyed those who had

5

*Signs of sadness*

authority, whereas the modern trend is to obey those who have power.

Today, we follow those who have power to shout the loudest and reach the greatest audience. For this reason the authors of television commercials have met with wonderful success in convincing the average housewife to purchase domestic appliances which she does not need and her husband to drive automobiles he cannot afford.

Our quick and easy response to those who have power is seen in the rapid change in women's and men's apparel. Not long ago millions of young girls began wearing miniskirts. That did not happen by accident or social chance. Somebody with power to control female fashions made a definite decision to introduce a new style, and immediately young women all over the world donned the mini. The irony of the matter is that they did not realize that they were being conned into doing what Mary Quant wanted rather than doing what they could have planned for themselves. In the near future the fads and fashions will change again. The hemline will go down or up if that is possible, and again the multitudes will flock to serve and obey whoever has power to shout the loudest and convince the greatest number.

Who will obey those in authority? Authority comes from God, consequently it does not corrupt. It is always lawful. It is always visible and recognizable. A king is known by his crown and the sheriff by his silver star. It is a deplorable reaction of human nature that the moment we are faced with authority we try to assert our independence by refusing to obey. We regard those in authority as people who are in competition against us. Our reaction to authority frequently betrays a feeling of inferiority. Like Lucifer of old we refuse to serve.

When it comes to power and the men who hold power over us through the mass media of the press, radio and movie screen, we experience no sense of inferiority because we do not know them. No man feels inferior to one he does not know. By operating in incognito fashion the purveyors of power are careful not to wear any badge or uniform that would prompt us to recognize them and refuse to obey them. It is not those with power who are entitled to our obedience, but only those who hold authority.

Another source of confusion of which many people are oblivious is the operation of an organized strategy that is designed to give local police force a bad name. Have you not noticed that as soon as the police arrive on a scene of disorder, the air is filled with cries of "POLICE BRUTALITY" or similar protests? That kind of conduct is carefully calculated to give the police a foul name. The moment one convinces the people of any community that the disciplinary measures of the police are being deployed against them, he strikes down the very keystone of law and liberty.

It is the function of the police to protect your peace, your person, and your property. By effectively paralyzing the instruments of order and peace, the enthronement of anarchy is assured, and under that anarchy no democracy can survive. The infiltration of wolves in the clothing of sheep often goes unnoticed because it bears some relatively innocuous name such as the Primrose Peace Foundation or the like.

Another issue of concern is the evidence of increasing disrespect for family unity. The role of family life as the basic unit of American society is being questioned. The fact that we cannot claim the wisdom to answer that questioning should not prevent us from discussing it.

I once heard the story of a middle-aged mother, who after observing the ingratitude of her son, decided that he no longer desired or deserved her care and attention. In the face of such deplorable conduct the dear lady could only say, "If that's how he feels about me he is no longer my son." Sad that she should feel like that because the ingratitude of her boy was only apparent. Deep in his heart he still loved her and needed her as before. The explanation of his thoughtless behavior is clear enough. Within him his own personality was rapidly changing, urging him to be independent, to rely on himself, to undertake responsibility, to terminate the habit of seeking others to solve his problems. It is

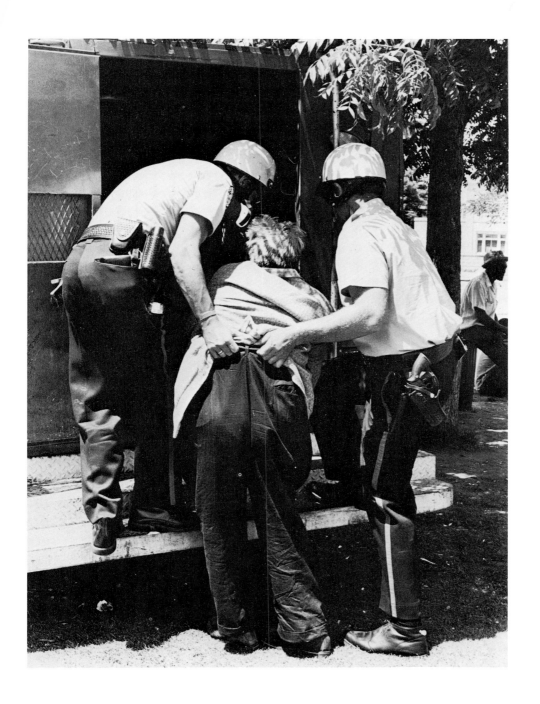

*The air is filled with cries of "POLICE BRUTALITY"*

characteristic of every normal boy. Eventually these traits of in-
dependence will lead to maturity, but until they do, the growing
boy is rather destitute and has little to rely on save his every un-
certain and incomprehensible self. We must not suppose that
youth's longing to be free is a sign that advice and friendship are
no longer required.

Adolescence is difficult for the young. Its powers are so new
and pungent that we can hardly expect a teenager to have full
and immediate control over them. We must allow a period of
adjustment.

The adolescent seeks our approval. He wants to know what
action to take and what course to follow. Unless we are vigilant,
he is forced to follow the crowd of his peers because the com-
panionship of like to like provides security, be it true or false.
Another boy may choose to imitate the adults of his environ-
ment on the basis that he can't get into too much trouble if he
goes only as far as they.

A strongwilled boy will decide for himself. It may be that his
decision is not always the best decision, but if we accept it for
what it is worth and give credit, if credit is due, then we foster
initiative and lessen his need for guidance. But we cannot estab-
lish such happy relations unless we maintain points of contact
and keep open the channels of communication.

There is much wisdom in the old maxim that two heads are
better than one. This being so, it naturally follows that dialogues
are usually better than monologues. It is more rewarding to
share the views of others than to insist that others be converted
to our own. If we are really sincere in seeking a solution to the
problem of generation communication, then we must ready our-
selves to begin building a bridge over the gulf which separates
the young from the old. That bridge must have points of contact
with both sides. It must support two-way traffic so that each
generation can travel at least half way. The foundation of that
bridge must be respect for the opinions of others, for it must
bear the heavy burden of two people who are working to-

10

*Keep open the channels of communication*

gether to reciprocate their covictions, to consider their thoughts, to understand their anxieties, to tolerate their emotions, and to share the few joys we still have in this world.

Building such bridges is not an easy matter. Progress is determined not by hope but by our effort and sincerity. We must be willing to work hard and long, since it will surely demand great dedication to lay the first gangplank. It is to our advantage that we do not know where and when to begin.

Tomorrow at breakfast we might say "Good morning" because it is amazing how many of us behave as though God made mothers for the sole purpose of fixing cereal and cheese. If a boy's father would read his post after his coffee and toast, he might discover that his children have something they wish to share with him even at that early our. The breakfast table can be a cafe-counter where everybody is doing exactly the same thing, but doing it alone. Or it can be the first plank of the bridge where parents and children meet to share as they eat.

The greatest thing we can do for a child is to show him at breakfast that he has as much to give us during the day as we have to give him. No compensation can make up for lack of communication. If familial relations are based on communication rather than on competition, then it is possible to introduce a new order of living in which good-will and good-relations prevail. Happiness doesn't just happen to your home. The people who live in your house must work to make happiness happen. A good mechanic does not say "I can't fix this auto." He tries, he practices, he works at it until he can.

It is erroneous to say that economic prosperity or pills will heal the many ills of mankind. Human nature demands something much more profound than monetary of medical assistance to heal its broken spirit. The problems engendered by war and poverty are so numerous that our generation cannot possibly provide completely for their solution. The most we can do, and by so doing we would surely do a great deal, is to maintain a vigilant interest in "guarding each man's dignity and saving each man's pride.'' By working together and as individuals, we can improve our customs and culture, and dispel the dismal signs of sadness.

13

# Responsible Re-Orientation

Childhood, adolescence, middle age and old age are the four cycles that constitute the normal life span of man. Generally speaking, the conduct of a child is determined by feeling and organic need. When the child matures to adolescence, his activity is controlled by concepts and choice, by intellect and will. Ambition that is flavored with respect marks middle age. Avarice strikes down the soul of the old man unless he has learned how to pray. Every person in every family possesses a particular physical and psychic make-up. Each stage of man's growth has its own peculiar characteristics, its own ups and downs, its own victories and defeats. Age gives each one a special role and a special identity.

Each generation has much to offer the other. Differences of opinion, differences of thought and ambition must be directed toward the emancipation of each one's creative talents and not toward the creation of tensions and tears or humiliations and fears. A family can live only by sharing ideas and experiences. Intolerance between members of any household brings only decay and death. People who live in the same house and share the same table must be united in mutual respect. A household that lacks mutual respect is not a family but only a barbarian tribe that is held together by bigotry and blood.

By refusing to respect others, we force them to conclude that they are unwanted and undesired, and so they run away to weirdie-beardie disaffiliated groups, there to discuss their "thing" in the context and comfort of a love-in.

It is the law of Christ that we would love one another. If we had love, one for another, we would be free from the restrictions that we impose on ourselves by selfishness, jealously and pride. Saint Paul wrote to the Corinthians:

*Each generation has much to offer the other*

*You must want love more than anything else—love is patient and kind; it is never jealous; it is never boastful or conceited; it is never rude or selfish; it does not take offence and it is not resentful.*

It is this love we need in our homes, because the home is the natural habitat of man. The beauty of the house, or its value in real estate, or even the social status of parents is not the essential property of a happy home. What people look for in their home is acceptance and affection. That is why there should always be a welcome for them. Home is the safe harbor, the base of love and the source of security, to which every member of the family unhesitantly turns. It is the place where each one finds his own flesh and blood waiting to make him feel wanted in order to complete the family circle.

Since teenagers are most sensitive about their friends, it is imperative that their friends be given the utmost respect and courtesy in the home. If this is not assured, then they will meet in places outside observation and control. The affection and understanding that your house provides for your children must be such that they will feel free and confident to discuss their problems. Do not allow your home to become a place where every sense of emotion and elation is crushed or immediately dethroned.

Besides a good home, a teenager also needs a good friend, in order to overcome the barriers established by confusion and fear. Every adolescent needs a faithful friend in whom to confide. If properly disposed, a loving father or mother can make the best friend of all. Only two qualities are required, and they are sincerity and understanding. Do not pretend to be a "Buddy," for pretence is easily detected. What you must be is a parachute that will cushion every fall and will bring your child safely to stand on his own feet. Every boy and girl needs someone who does not change, someone who is always there, someone who can still believe when all others lose trust.

As children of God each of us are brothers; each one is equal:

> *A dispute arose between them about which should be reckoned the greatest. But, He said to them the greatest among you must behave as if he were the least, the leader as if he were the one who serves. For who is the greater; the one at table or the one that serves? The one at table surely? Yet here am I among you as one who serves.*

That is what we read in the Christian Scriptures.

This same lesson is found in the Buddhist Scriptures:

> *A family is a place where a mind lives with other minds. If these minds love each other, the home will be as beautiful as a flower garden. But if these minds get out of harmony with each other, it is like a storm that plays havoc with a garden. If disharmony rises within one's family, one should not blame others but should examine his own mind and follow the right path.*

This equality approach—if I may call it that—will demand a departure from ancient attitudes that are now obsolete. It necessitates responsible re-orientation. It is unwise to pursue any course

18

of conduct or of control that is no longer relevant. The modern complex way of life presents for our consideration a challenging situation that was unknown in former times. We must accept the fact that precedent and experience, though always important, are no longer sufficient guides.

Parents may never again pattern the lives of their children solely on the memory of their own childhood, however sacred or pleasant that memory may be. It is true that the men and women of my father's generation made greater technological advancement than was achieved in the three thousand years that preceded this century, but it is also clear that the children of today will attain even more spectacular results. Unbidden of the words of the song come claimant to mind:

> *I hear babies cry, I watch them grow;*
> *They'll learn more than I'll ever know.*

In a letter to youth, Archbishop Helder of Recife wrote:

> *You will land on the planets; you will see the end of the armaments race and of war; not because of idealism but because of a realistic acceptance of the absurdities, you will right the wrongs; you will accomplish the socialization that can best serve man.*

The glory of the past does not solve the problems facing us today, and we shall not solve them, either, unless we are willing

1" />

to conceive and bring to fruition a new concept of brotherhood that is not only moral and modern but adequate and acceptable as well. What we are as a nation today, and what we contribute to other nations has been bestowed on us by farsighted men who looked to the future as well as to the past in their speculation of every right and privilege we now possess.

Author Leon Rovetta has warned us that the present way of life requires the development of individual self-control in order to minimize the need of external control. Our children are on wheels, they are on their own, they are "on the loose." The average teen-age American boy receives approximately Seven Hundred Dollars per year either from work or pocket-money or both combined. It is good to teach young people the value of money and how to make money because that instills initiative and leads to success in later life. But, reports from the business world reveal that very little of our young people's money is wisely spent.

Teenagers represent 9% of our population, but they purchase 16% of the cosmetics, 45% of the soft drinks, 24% of the watches, 20% of the radios, and 30% of the cameras sold in the United States. Last year American girls spent more than two billion dollars on clothing, and 18% of our boys bought automobiles. It is the knowledge of these things that prompts the suggestion that if we were willing to give more love and affection, we would not be forced to give more money and incur more debt.

Let's suppore that your son is a senior in high-school. His report cards are good. He is popular with his peers. His record is clean. You are justly proud of your son. Yesterday he learned history, equations, and social science. Today, he is ready to graduate. Has he all the answers? What does he know about you? What does he know about himself?

Does he know how to take his place in his community? Has he been taught how to love people? Does he know that every person is a reflection of God and that he has something to learn from every person that he will ever meet?

In the world many people want to say "I am an individual."

*What does he know about himself*

There is challenge in that, but so, too, there is caution. Individuality is not a lesson that is learned in school, but a right that is earned in life. Unless your boy has discovered that every man is an individual he has denied the individuality of himself. And what about tomorrow when your son fastens his military tunic and hears only about the rights that are won by the fury of guns and the force of war? It is an occasion for concern because it is a matter of contradiction.

By a process of contradiction we have alienated and frustrated those who are young. We tell a young boy that he must behave as a man, and minutes later when he seeks permission to do something new—something we have never done ourselves—we deny him the opportunity to undertake responsibility. Forever we admonish the young, "Don't drink, don't smoke, don't get pregnant." Then we proceed to do all these things to amuse our own dull-hours.

We put guns in the hands of boys and command them to fight for their country, but we deny them the right to vote. It is a contradiction to say, "You are old enough to defend, but not old enough to define." Like the over-protective mother, this "Great Society" that emphasizes the advantage of being young has estranged large numbers of young people from the sacred values and traditions of their ancestors.

We need to refocus our viewpoints on life. We need a clear picture of reality. As we look to the past with reverence and respect, let us not fear to face the future with reflection and responsibility. Responsibility means the ability to respond to duty, and surely we have a responsibility to bear for proliferating the market with magazines and movies that foster only immorality and illicit adventure. The law attributes 18% of all crime committed in the United States to those who have not reached their twentieth year. But the law does not recognize the right of our young people to protection from the phenomenon of pornography that propagates profanity and promiscuity.

On Sunday, March 23, 1969, a teenage "Crusade for Decency in

It is a matter of contradiction

Entertainment" drew a crowd of 30,000 to the Orange Bowl Stadium in Miami. The teenagers organized the crusade to repudiate the conduct of a well known singer who had been charged with indecent exposure at a concert in Miami on March 1. The rally was promoted by a steering committee of ten members representing different faiths and schools in and around Miami.

Is it any wonder that there are long hairs and short skirts in protestation of our indifferences to serious abuse? Which of us took action when the president of a large university informed his governor that the function of a university president consists in "providing parking for the faculty, football for the alumni and sex for students"?

Around the globe fault is attributed to collegians who refuse to base their careers on stable institutions and programs. I do not condone all the tactics and acrobatics of those who rebel in violence against what they see and hear. Yet I dare say that it is to our benefit that someone is protesting against the present order, because too many believe that everything is "hunky-dory" in this climate of make-belief, fantasy, and fun. It would indeed be sad if youth's endeavor to sharpen our sensitivities, or the disturbances they cause by knocking at the doors of our conscience should generate only the censure and condemnation of society. It is true that young people protest and demand, but how can we blame them in this world of injustice, insecurity, and war? It is judicious to remember that it is not always the other person who is in need of reform. Before reforming others, let us reform ourselves.

Reformation of its nature requires education. Fathers and mothers are obliged to give their children as good a start in life as they received themselves. The ideal is to do even better, because in this way the progress of civilization is assured. By the end of this century the population of the United States is expected to pass the 300 million mark, so that it is urgently necessary that we re-assess the duty of parents in the field of education. They receive from nature a primary mandate in this area.

*Let us reform ourselves*

Consequently, the career of a child depends largely on the ability and willingness of his parents to do something about it. That does not mean that a man must know as much Greek as his son, but it does mean that he should keep a close eye on modern developments. It may even mean abandoning ideas once learned in 1940, if they are no longer valid.

During the depression, for example, not many had access to a car. Today, the situation has changed. Having a car is far more common than having a poodle. Many teenagers have cars of their own, and many teenage activities take place in a car such as watching a movie or listening to the stereo. Each year new teenage drivers get behind the wheel. It is a big event because we have made the automobile a symbol of freedom and power. What is surprising, however, is that we have failed to teach the average American boy how to drive. That is the only conclusion we find in the hospital and cemetery records. We have been so busy telling our youth that having power is exciting that we have forgotten to say that having control of power is even more exciting.

In this matter of education we must learn from our students before they will learn from us. We must fill them with confidence in us before we can teach them to have confidence in themselves. It is our duty to provide, not to prevent. A man cannot have new thoughts if his training prevents him from having a mind of his own. It is the function of teachers not only to give a chapter of facts and figures but also to find with each student an identity that is concretely evident and relevant. In other words, to deny the individuality of any pupil is to deny his real value and total worth.

If it is in your heart to pardon repetition, then hear it again, because whenever a group of people agree on anything, only one of them is usually necessary. The theory of the cynic which warns us that ideas that are new are not true, or that ideas that are true are not new, has no place in circles of learning. Education is complete only when it draws out the personality of each child and fashions it until he becomes interesting, eloquent, and at the same time, sincere. Education does not of necessity make a man rich, but it always makes him precious.

It is only when we teach our students to formulate new ideas of their own that they can contribute something new, something original, something this world has never known. Let us be wary lest we incur the contempt that deservedly falls on any race that values only what is old while neglecting to discover what yet remains unknown. I dare say that the greatest evil that Communism inflicts is that its common schools produce common citizens who think and talk instinctively in the same manner. That is why in Christian California young boys and girls are trained to be individuals, but in Communist countries the Red Guard has sought to produce a standardization of citizens in much the same way we produce standard sewing machines and chewing gum.

Realizing the importance of drawing forth the intellectual and individual potential of young children, parents ought to introduce them to the practice of good reading. If possible, books and magazines that are suitable to each one's age ought to be available throughout the house. There will be reading assignments given at school, but apart from these, it is wise to make children familiar with the local library from their earliest years and to reward every inclination to browse there.

Men who hold public office would do their constituents a good service by providing decent social halls and places of mental and physical edification. I am not suggesting that city or county boards replace or supplant the home, for that is a fundamental cell of human society. But some assistance is necessary, especially where children are obliged to rely on extra familial facilities.

It is becoming increasingly difficult to provide any student with personal or individual education. Centralization of educational facilities has become an accepted part of American life. The policy of centralization in any department provides the opportunity to avail of specialized services, but it must not become so absolute an obsession as to make us lose sight of the essential end for which it is designed, because it also produces some ill-effects.

27

Chief among these is the growth of large institutions where people are herded together far distant from their families and friends. As a single worker in a very large company loses his individual identity in the massive sea of employees, so too, the student of today's university and tommorow's megaversity can be known only by the series of holes in his computer card. It may be that forms of such sophisticated administration enable college authorities to prepare concise documentation on their mulitudinous enrollment, but the inevitable consequence of such mechanical operations is the emergence of a system that can not provide any student with special attention.

In church circles there is an increasing acceptance of the theory that smaller parishes provide better services for the people. If this is the case, and I have reason to believe it is, having some knowledge of the impact of that apostolate, then it would be better for us to stem the tide that brings large numbers of rural boys and girls to our cities in quest of academic training and skills.

Students who migrate to cities for educational purposes tend to remain in them for life. In 1930 approximately 60% of the American people lived on the land. Today 82% of our citizens live in towns and cities. This lack of balance in the location of our population causes frustration in urban areas and lack of employment in smaller communities. Compare the solid stability of American life forty years ago with the present instability of congested campuses, apartments, and offices, and you may discover that overcrowded institutions do not inspire a love for learning.

The mind of man functions best when it is free from distraction, and the formation of character is more readily induced by calmer surroundings.

In the Orient the modern trend in education is directed towards the development of numerous small colleges. In England and France, newly organized societies are devoting themselves to the formation of private schools that are being attended by the most fastidious classes of European society. Should it be said that while other countries were making intelligent efforts to provide

*Lack of balance in the location of our population causes frustrations*

unfrustrated facilities, we in the United States neglected the very life-blood of our nation and the living medium of our distinctive reputation as a nation?

Education that seeks to reform must be based on the preservation of family life, which in turn is founded on the Law of God. The re-orientation and preservation of family life is assured only when fathers and mothers direct their own lives according to the Divine Law and impress upon their children that this is the only yardstick they consider appropriate at all times. If parents would keep the Law of God, they would be surprised how often their children would manifest sincere gratitude to them for saying and doing what they themselves were sometimes afraid or ashamed to say and do. When we consider—that 35% of the world's people will be under 15 within the next 20 years, we are keenly aware of man's duty to instill in his children strong convictions of moralty and sincerity.

While it is true that we should not sacrifice our own generation for the sake of posterity, we are obliged to set the stage for our children and for our children's children. Although the actuarial tables indicate that we may contemplate singing in the choirs of angels by the end of the century, we dare not dispense ourselves of our duty to contribute something to society so that this world will be a better place for man to live in when that time comes. It is only by satisfying this obligation that we can hope for responsible re-orientation.

# Alone in the Woods

Have you ever walked alone in the woods? Going into the woods is indeed a special experience, especially if you go alone. In every wood there is the opportunity to get away for awhile from the monotony of life. Daily duties, however satisfying or rewarding they may be, sooner or later lose their zest. Even the common companionships of life, however interesting they may be, become temporarily dull. The blues set in and with them the enervating staleness of disquiet and discontent. In such moods it is refreshing to find peace and solitude in the rarefied atmosphere of the woods. The woodland has its own magic, and in its surroundings it is impossible to abstract the mind from the significance of God's artistry, His majestic creations, and the concept of His Eternal Law that is irresistible, absolute, and indefeasible.

One day in the woods while musing about these things I was suddenly startled by a nearby sound. Surely a squirrel I thought, but then I saw the picture of peace personified. There was a girl there, pure as a baby. Her personality rather than her picture has lingered poetically in my mind.

*On a mossy bank she sat—*
*A pretty child of summers few.*
*Copper-beech her curly hair,*
*Her eyes were speedwells blue.*

*And she hummed a little song,*
*As she strung her daisy chain.*
*Such a lovely elfin sprite,*
*Singing such a sweet refrain.*

*Then a sunbeam straying far,*
*Kissed the copper-beech brown hair;*
*Glistened on the curly locks,*
*And burnished gold a halo there.*

*Though her dress was faded blue,*
*And her little feet were bare;*
*What a winsome maid she was,*
*With copper-sunbeam-burnished hair.*

*"Who are you my little maid?"*
*At the sound she raised her head;*
*Smilingly, she looked at me.*
*"I'm Lou, the unknown child," she said.*

*Again she strung her daisy chain,*
*As she sung her lilting song.*
*Tapping twinkling feet the while;*
*A gleam of heaven in her smile.*

What a fortunate distraction, what a charming discovery, what a profound lesson this little girl could teach. She was unknown. Her parents were lost in the large world of frustration and fear.

*Have you ever walked alone in the woods?*

Would that she could find them to show them that there is another side to the coin of family life.

It is the side that requires children to respect their parents. The contemporary world is fully aware of the duty of parents to their children, but it seems to forget that children have a duty to their parents. In modern society the emphasis is on youth. The influence we allow our young people to exert on our daily lives is enormous. The tones of our radios and records, the beat of our songs and the rhythm of our dances, the style of our clothing, the standard of our education and industry, even the new-look of our politics and religion are all largely determined by the mind and fancy of almost twenty million teenagers now residing within our frontiers.

The fact is that our stress on youth programs has relegated many parents to the scrap-heap. Society is over-concerned with age limits. The upper age bracket is being gradually lowered. Positions of employment in state and private agencies are being denied to our elders, not because they are incompetent but because they are old. It is understandable that men must be recruited young for the purpose of training, longevity of service, and in order to enable them to qualify for pension programs. The fact that a young man is able and willing to give good service does not mean that his elders should be considered redundant. Children must reciprocate the respect they demand of their parents.

A young person cannot claim to be a loyal child of God if he is not first loyal to his parents. It is easy to be insensitive to the cares and concerns of parents. Indifference is particularly harsh when parents are old. There are problems in senility as well as in adolescence. Unlike his children, the old man must face the burden of loneliness, declining health, and at times the loss of his deceased spouse. As the body loses its agility, tiredness sets in. Ideas that have been set are not easily changed. We accuse our elders of frustrating the world by teaching us too much, too quickly. It has taken five or six thousand years to develop the culture we now enjoy. We have matured slowly from the point

*On the Giri*

of using our fingers to eat to the conventional culture of cutlery and cups. But that progress did not happen overnight. It required centuries of formation. Our parents are part of that culture, and we can not expect to change them all at once.

There is no time in a man's life when compassion and understanding are more necessary than in his old age. The possibility that those who are old will make mistakes is inevitable, but this is no reason for denying them understanding. The process of understanding your father and mother begins in your own heart. The original sin of our first parents darkened our understanding, weakened our willpower, and left in us a strong inclination to evil. As children of God we seek what is good, but as children of Adam we seek what is bad.

Because there is in the heart of everyone a conflict between good and evil, it requires constant care to do good and avoid evil. In the city of Rome there is a famous painting of two young men each of whom is holding a globe of the world in his right hand. Their names are well known in history as Alexander the Great and Saint Aloysius Gonzaga. The artist has portrayed them alike except that Alexander is pictured in tears while Aloysius is the picture of peace and joy.

Alexander was one of the greatest Generals of recorded history. As King of Macedonia he conquered Persia, Egypt and India. But while he conquered the world around him he failed to conquer the turmoil in his own heart. In the city of Babylon he died a drunkard's death at the age of thirty-two.

Aloysius, on the otherhand, lived in poverty all his life. It was his care to remain uncontaminated by the vanity and splendour that attended the court of his father, Ferdinand, Marquis of Castiglione. Aloysius conquered no empires but he died in peace because he had learned to conquer himself.

What does it profit a man to conquer the world if he fails to conquer himself?

Unless we succeed in bringing the conflict in our own hearts under control and learning to understand ourselves, we cannot understand our parents. It is only by knowing ourselves and understanding ourselves that we can know and understand our parents. Self-knowledge is the beginning of understanding others.

Not many people know themselves because only a few have the courage to face the dismal implications of their own values. The prerequisites of knowing yourself are courage and a willingness to learn.

Courage is a virtue of many dimensions. It embraces the entire circle of human conduct. Like a prism that reflects all the colors of the rainbow according to its setting, so too courage reveals the various characteristics of man in relation to the adversity of his circumstances and the enormity of his goals. Moral courage refers to the integrity of men whose conduct is always in accord with their conscience.

We shall concern ourselves now with another aspect of courage. We shall consider the courage of the adventurer who does not fear to launch out into the unknown and unchartered zodiac of self-examination.

Imagine that you are standing on the uppermost cliff of the seashore. Above, you behold the limitless sky and below, the endless depth of the deep. You are not enclosed or confined. You are free as a bird, and if you have initiative and imagination, you shall find wings to fly. Fly far away. Fly around and above the little world of egotism in which you have been imprisoned for so long. As you fly, observe below the cozy nest you have been building for yourself to the exclusion of others. It takes courage to leave the nest and to extricate oneself from the myopic seclusion of security. Have you the courage to fly?

The second prerequisite of knowing yourself is the willingness to learn. To illustrate this point I recall the story of the young man who wished to become a monk. Having entered the monastery, the young man was invited by the abbot to a cup of tea. The young fellow was a loquacious individual, for he was so busy talking about himself that he had not so much as taken a mouthful of tea. His cup remained full to the brim. Meanwhile the abbot, having finished his cup, desired to have another. He offered to pour his guest some more tea. But the young man said, "Father Abbot, my cup is still full. If you pour any more, you shall spill the tea that is now in my cup." In reply the abbot said to him, "My friend, unless you are willing to empty yourself of what you have, you will never be able to receive abundantly of that which is apart from you."

It is generally admitted that the qualities of youth are innocence, enthusiasm, and love. To meet young people who possess these characteristics is a rewarding and refreshing experience. They do not hope for happiness because it is already a radiant reality of life. Yet you know that many young people are most unhappy. If you frequent the places where teenagers meet, you will encounter some who are delinquent, desperate, and despised.

Why, you ask, is life a paradox? What makes people lonely, confused, and sad? Why are 45 million Americans affected by alcoholism? Why do one thousand teenagers steal automobiles in the United States everyday? Why do people resort to drugs and dope? What drives people into the world of make-belief where their hopes of escaping reality are shattered and destroyed? The confused society is composed of many people, and no two of them are alike.

Each one has a special problem. Special problems require special answers. Since all men share the same nature, we can make a general observation. The source of youthful heartbreak can usually be traced to the loss of the qualities of youth. Those who lose their innocence suffer the plague of a guilty conscience. Those who lose enthusiasm yield to despair because they lack a sense of purpose of life. Those who have not love are torn by jealousy and self-pity.

While there is no magic formula to transform torture into tranquility, yet in most cases peace can be restored and the broken spirit can be renewed. The secret is to give man another chance. Picture a little boy breaking a rubber ball to see what is inside of it. Having destroyed his treasured possession, he finds only empty air. By normal standards his action is foolish. But that little

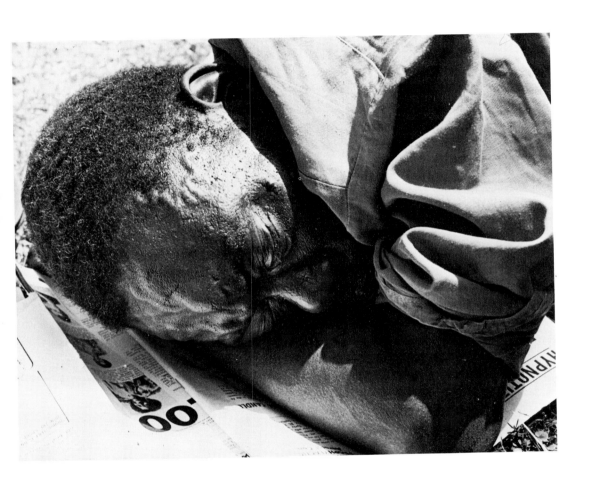

*Those who lose enthusiasm yield to despair*

boy has learned a valuable lesson. If he is given another chance, another rubber ball, he will not repeat his mistake. In the same way those who are unhappy must seek and receive the opportunity to try again.

If you would help a friend who suffers the severe pain of psychological illness or unhappiness, do not condemn him. You may be justified in condemning the circumstances and the people of his environment, but you have no right to condemn the person, himself. Neither will punishment solve the problem. Rehabilitation and understanding provide the only solution.

In rehabilitating those who are emotionally disturbed, it is important to put before their minds the importance of spiritual assistance. I do not recommend the occult sciences of witchcraft and black magic. These may be growing popular among those who are seeking solutions to problems of frustration, but they do not provide true answers. There is only one true answer—and that is God. Exclude God and discover that life has no meaning. God is the author of life. He loves all men. He can help all men.

The value of spiritual assistance cannot be exaggerated. Many young people have already discovered this fact for themselves. Recently, it was brought to my attention that teenagers are turning to different forms of the Buddhist religion. Buddhism emphasizes the necessity of self-discipline and frequent meditation to renunciate what one is inordinately attached to. There is wisdom in that philosophy.

Christianity, too, stresses the need for discipline, prayer, and reflection. Indeed, Christianity goes further than Buddhism. Notice how pictures of the Buddha depict him with closed eyes. On the other hand, have you ever seen a picture of the Christ in which His eyes were not wide open? Forever looking intently inwards will not solve the problems of one who must live with others. Man must examine himself, and having done so, he must open his eyes to face the reality of himself, his peers, and his parents.

Someday you must walk in the woods, alone and close to God. While you are there think about your father and mother. How

*Phsychological illness or unhappiness*

do you relate to them? Do you make them happy or sad? Are you one of those people who suffer from a kind of occular deficiency by which they see only the faults of their parents and are unable to see their own? It is significant that the faults we see in our parents are precisely the faults that we have ourselves.

Remember the Fourth Commandment "Honor your Father and your Mother"—sounds almost like General McArthur's farewell to West Point: "Duty, Honor, Country." In his address to the men of the army, McArthur pointed out that every soldier must go beyond the call of duty; he must give more than obedience; he must render respect. The Fourth Commandment obliges us not only to obey our parents, but also to honor them. It obliges us to be gracious and kind, always ready to help and happy to serve.

The Chinese have a saying:

> *When I see the sacred liao wo, (the symbol of parenthood) my thoughts return to those who gave me birth, raised me, and now are tired. I would repay the affection they have shown me, but it is as the sky; it can never be reached.*

That philosophy is far removed from the American institution known as the rest-home. The old like the young thrive best at home amongst their relatives and friends. It is easy to stay young at heart if allowed to stay with those who are still young. Spending a million dollars on your father's funeral will not compensate him for the affection he should be receiving now.

One of the most misued words in the world is the word LOVE. Crooners croon it, pop-singers, if I may coin a word, popit, and guitars wail and moan around it every time it occurs in a song. Today, indeed, millions of men and women talk, write, and sing about love. So it is rather important that we pause and ask ourselves what is love?

What does love for parenthood mean? It is a virtue of two dimensions—an awareness of one's own debt of gratitude and an affection that leads to effective action for the good of others. It is an attitude to life that was fully lived by a noted figure in French history who endeared himself to his master by replying to every request in these words: "My Lord, if it is possible, you may consider it done; if it is impossible, we shall see."

Bobby Sherman, the star of "Here Come The Brides," has given us an inspiring message when he said, "I have groovy folks. They are totally in love with each other. I hope that I can be like that. They are more like my friends, so we all go out to dinner together." You, too, can have parents that are friends. Are you willing to go with them to dinner?

It may be that our ancestors did not leave us the perfect legacy, or inspire the perfect heritage, but what they had, we received, and it has shaped our destiny. Listen to the words of the ancient toast:

Here's to the old stock, the brave stock, the bold stock
The Fathers and Mothers who bore us—
To their courage unending—their spirit unbending
That lighted the pathway before us.

Theirs was the gentle heart living their life apart,
Far from the tinsel and glory;
Seeking no tawdry frame—proud of an honest name
Simple their unwritten story.

Brave was the soul of them, stalwart the whole of them,
Knowing the wrong from the right,
Despair never bowed them, defeat never cowed them;
Game to the end of the fight.

So here's to the old stock, the brave stock, the bold stock
Though the grave or the years may divide,
'Til the end of the way, 'til the close of our day
We will remember with pride.

44

# Games With God

The celebrated author, Doctor Eric Berne, has told us of games, very serious little games, people play with each other every day. In the psychology of human affairs and communication men and women are forever playing games for some selfish motive. Human activity is often determined by ulterior purposes. This is the case when a man conducts himself in a certain way in hopes of gaining a favor or advantage.

In a similar fashion mankind plays games with God. These games we play with the Divine can be called religion. Religion consists of man's effort to communicate with God and thereby attain the fullness of life. The word "Divine" stands for a power that is superior to man and is the ultimate cause of all things, both active and passive. Some men believe that there is only one God. Others say that there are many gods.

Christ said that there is only one God, and in Him there are three Divine Persons, really distinct and equal in every way. According to some, God cannot die while others believe that God is already dead. Jesus Christ revealed that God always was and always will be. Those of us who endeavor to communicate with God do so in search of happiness in this world, and eternal life in the next. Our communication with God is now dulled in the obscurity of faith, but after death we shall communicate with God in eternal light.

Long before recorded history began, man lived in a world of fear. We are all afraid of the unknown. A soldier is afraid to take a bomb in his hand if he does not know how to dismantle it.

In the early days of our history our ancestors lived in constant fear of the sun and storms. For early man life was hazardous and full of peril. It seemed that there was no escape from the dangers of nature. In his desperate fear man came to believe in a supernatural force which had control over all things. Unable to change

*Religion consists of man's effort to communicate with God*

the world around him, early man acknowledged the existence of the Divine. Man's first notion of God was that of a most powerful supernatural being. His first dealings with God were based on fear.

After a lapse of so many years it is now almost impossible, although we presently examine religion as we do the other sciences, to describe precisely the circumstances that moved our ancestors to communicate with God for the first time. Many scholars are of the opinion that our early religious experience was directed towards the society or tribe rather than to the individual. The spirit and feeling that religion evoked was found only when all members of the clan participated in the tribal rites. These were ceremonies performed in accordance with a prescribed ritual. The emphasis was on God's dealings with the people rather than with the person. From this primitive but ecumenical awareness we have inherited many sacred signs and traditions that give solidarity to society.

Religion taught the individual the importance of giving consideration to the needs of others. The advent and acceptance of religious morals proved to be a key factor in the formation of our society. From the religion of his tribe each individual member absorbed a sense of moral values that was directed towards the well-being of his total community. Religion became the service of intelligent individuals of a community to the supernatural power that has full control over their immediate desires and final destinies. Religion presupposes a Divine object that is independent of man.

In the Christian Religion that Divine Object is God. He is the beginning and the end of all things. He alone is the supreme reality of life. He is the source of life, truth, and love. He is behind all that happens, "reaching from end to end, regulating all things sweetly." And yet God is not easily discovered. Only one eye can see Him, and that is the eye of Faith. Faith can penetrate the external form of visible things and behold the reality of the invisible God. Christianity is a series of beliefs and behaviors that direct our entire lives to God.

So astonishing has been the growth and spread of Christianity that almost one third of the world's population now offers worship to Christ. In round figures there are approximately 990 million Christians in the world today. Not all of these, however, profess the same faith or practice the same ritual. The Christian world is divided into many sects. Of these the Catholic Church is the largest. Its membership of Six Hundred Million outnumbers all other Christian denominations.

The world into which Christ was born was governed by the Roman emperor, whose prefectures and governors controlled a vast empire comprising forty provinces. Rome was the capital city and had within its walls the residence of the emperor and the federal buildings. From the City of Rome the emperor ruled his mighty kingdom. His best friends were well paid to watch over his imperial interests throughout the provinces, collect taxes, guard his possessions, execute his laws, and maintain a large army which served with unquestioned loyalty his every command. At the provincial level, the paid representative of Rome took precedence over the local or native authorities.

Centuries of Roman diplomacy and military conquest had won for the emporer the final say in all matters both judicial and administrative concerning the welfare of the empire. Add to this the religious cult whereby the cities of each province employed delegates at their provincial capital to offer solemn worship to the emperor, and it is easy to understand how the Roman Emperor became the absolute monarch of all he surveyed. This was the system which the apostles were determined to change and to put in its place the Kingdom and the Teachings of Christ.

The leader of the apostolic band was Peter. Peter was a fisherman. He was a fiery soul and sometimes brave. He wanted to die for Christ but changed his mind when a young working girl looked him straight in the eye. But in the presence of his Lord, Peter could not hide his faith. He, it was, who cried, "Thou art the Christ." And it was he who drew his sword against those who would take his Master captive. Always himself and always human, Peter was the unpolished rock whom Christ elected to rule the infant Church.

Fifty days after the resurrection, Peter convoked a public meeting on the streets of Jerusalem. In his first address he drew the attention of the citizenry to the new found religion. The reaction of the crowd is described by Saint Luke:

Hearing this, they were cut to the heart and said to Peter and the apostles, "What must we do, brother?" "You must repent," Peter answered. "And every one of you must be baptized in the name of Jesus Christ for the forgiveness of your sins, and you will receive the gift of the Holy Spirit. The promise that was made is for you and your children, and for all those who are far away, for all those whom the Lord our God, will call to himself!" He spoke to them for a long time, using many arguments, and he urged them, "Save yourselves from this perverse generation!"

They were convinced by his arguments, and they accepted what he said and were baptized. That very day about three thousand were added to their number. These remained faithful to the teaching of the apostles, to the brotherhood, to the breaking of bread, and to the prayers.

The many miracles and signs worked through the apostles made a deep impression on everyone. The faithful all lived together and owned everything in common: they sold their goods and possessions and shared-out the proceeds among themselves according to what each one needed.

They went as a body to the temple every day but met in their houses for the breaking of bread; they shared their food gladly and generously; they praised God and were looked up to by everyone. Day by day, the Lord added to their community those destined to be saved.

Following that first Pentecost, Peter began to preach and baptize in the towns and villages of Judea, Samaria, and Galilee. Acting on behalf of Rome, Pontius Pilate had refused to acknowledge the innocence of Christ. Peter now resolved to bring the law of Christ to Rome. It was here that he reigned as first Pope. The city did not receive him, and about 65 A.D. he was crucified, by order of the Emperor Nero. The powers of Rome were not anxious to tolerate a group which demanded freedom to worship one who had been condemned to death by a Roman governor. In the mind of the emperor, the less organizations operating outside his control, the better.

Such groups were regarded with suspicion because of their weakening effects on the emperor's hold and authority. The infant church should not be accepted lest it loosen the imperial grip on the people. Instead it should be immolated and destroyed. This was the policy of the capital for more than two hundred years. The bill *Ad Bestias,* was passed to allow Roman governors to throw Christians to the wild beasts in the amphitheater. To this day the catacombs in Rome bear silent testimony of the gory measures adopted to execute the policy of the emperor. But in spite of this opposition, the church began to grow and expand. The Acts of the Apostles describe the missionary journeys of Saint Paul, and his success among the inhabitants of the Roman East.

Paul was a matchless organizer whose unwavering faith enabled him to conceive and bring to fruition vast schemes which to others less singularly gifted seemed impossible. Within a few years he managed to establish Christian communities in Salonika, Athens, Corinth, and Rome.

The first Christians were formed by the Apostles into a society and from that society came the development of Christ's teachings which we call theology. Before long the basic principles were written down. It was not unusual for Saint Paul to write letters to his converts in particular areas in which he explained certain truths or clarified some matters of doubt. The other apostles did likewise though not so often. Besides letters, short accounts of our Lord's life were also recorded. Of these accounts four were singled out as being the accurate and inspired word of God. They are called the Four Gospels and togther with the Acts of the Apostles and some of the above mentioned letters they make up the New Testament.

For the most part, Peter and Paul spent their lives as missionaries. Both of them traveled extensively throughout the East and along the shores of the Mediterranean. Their campaign consisted in setting up churches and preaching about Jesus who had been crucified for the sins of men. Steadily and in spite of official persecution, Christianity spread over the Mediterranean world. Unknown to themselves these first Christians were shaping not only their own destiny but the destiny of subsequent generations and the course of future world history.

From the beginning Christianity broke from the legal codes of Jerusalem and took to itself the culture and tradition of the Greeks. The Christian code was written in Greek before it was written in Latin. Even in our own time the Christian Ritual contains a generous supply of Greek terminology. The words *bishop, priest, deacon, church,* and many more come from the Greek and betray the amalgamation of Greek and Christian thought at an early stage.

By the second century, almost every town in the Mediterranean littoral could boast of accommodating its own Christian community. Today Christianity is the chief religion of Europe and America. The simple truths which demand love of God and love of one's fellowmen are the big attraction of the growing Church. In awe the Gentiles would say, "See these Christians, how they love one another."

The intellect of a Christian is challenged by a massive collection of truths about God and God's dealings with man. These truths are made known to us by reason and study, by speculation and revelation, and by the teachings and traditions of the church. The dogmas of our faith supply us with a rationale for living as we do. Christianity provides for man's faculty of free-will a series of precepts which must be observed in order to establish peace among men and to obtain for us eternal salvation. The observance of these precepts gives us a sense of values and an order of priorities.

But apart from satisfying the needs of man's intellect and will,

*Big attraction of the growing churches*

the Christian faith also offers him the opportunity of sharing immediately in the life of God by means of the liturgy. In the Christian cult, the sincere believer finds a sense-of-belonging which generates faith, keeps it alive, and prompts him to give it his frequent and faithful attention. Belief in the incarnation of God the Son, vivifies our love for Christ because His personality is more acceptable to us when it is experienced as corporeal as well as spiritual.

The historical fact that the apostles lived and spoke with Christ re-enforces our faith in Him and gives us the immediacy and tangibility of Divine love, which our human nature desires. The incarnation is not only a point of verification, but, it is also the visible and objective sign around which our faith evolves.

The complex process of religious ceremony is designed to enable man to communicate with God. Ritual of any form is most effective when those present are not merely passively attendant but deeply involved by active participation and commitment. A man cannot believe without participation no more than he can participate without belief.

These are thrilling times for the church. The Holy Spirit has filled the people of God with spiritual enthusiasm. Never before were bishops and priests so brave and willing to meet the needs of the people. In many instances, this has necessitated a departure from ancient structures which were once adequate but which are no longer relevant. For some the challenge of sharing responsibility is repugnant to the security they enjoyed when they were told precisely what action to take, what course to follow. Others have forgotten who holds authority and who it is we are bound to obey.

In such times and circumstances, it is beneficial to remember that the changes which are taking place and the progress that is being pursued are not miscalculated accidents of transition. These things have been carefully conceived in the mind of God who is asking us through His Church to bring them to fruition. It is the Father who has sent the Holy Spirit to work in us and to wake us up so that we can see His great plan as it unfolds in this period of history.

The church is still growing. The church is forever growing and we must not be surprised if we sometimes feel the aches of growing pains. When you look at the church, you do not see a closed book of doctrine and morality in which God has stated everything He wishes us to know. What you see is a growing organism that has not yet attained full maturity. The church is a pilgrim who has not reached his destination, but who is still struggling on because he believes in the promise of his Guide. In that sense the church depends on every person because God has called the people to preserve and share the faith.

Do you think that his call involves too much for you, or do you suppose that with God's grace, you could manage to renew your own faith and the faith of your friend? Keep in mind that renewal means much more than a re-declaration of Christian traditions. Renewal requires a new heart that is capable of giving life and pulsation to a community which is a living witness to Christ. Only then, will others see the value of Christianity. Only then, will others see that our faith is more than a game with God.

# The Price of Destiny

Long ago, primitive people had immediate recourse to food and to the raw materials that are necessary for life. Nowadays, that situation has changed because more people exist and their demands are in consequence greater. Modern man receives food and clothing for sustenance by using his time and talents in conjunction with the efforts of others. It is proper for man to work either for himself or with others, and thereby receive the reward for his endeavor.

If a man is incapable of work or of making any contribution to the well-being of himself or society, then the law of nature dictates that society should help him to help himself. On the other hand, if a man is able but refuses to work it is foolish for him to expect of others what he does not expect of himself.

In the context of work, we cannot survive alone without being limited, confined, and in a sense, imprisoned. But if we share our talents and cooperate with each other, then our horizons are broadened and our potential is proportionately increased. It is only by giving of ourselves that we have a right to receive. It is unfair to grasp the opportunities afforded by organized society if we refuse to accept the responsibilities that society imposes. Whenever a man is neglectful of his talents and abilities, he either loses his sense of purpose in life, or else he becomes the chronic subject of a guilt-complex. These make a man old before his time and usually terminate in some mental disorder or frustration.

Standing on the desk in my father's office, there is a bronze bust of President Theodore Roosevelt. On the base of the bust runs this inscription:

*I wish to preach, not the doctrine of
ignoble case,
But the doctrine of strenuous life.
The life of toil and effort, of labor
and strife;
To preach that highest form of success
that comes,
Not to the man who desires mere ease
and peace,
But to the man who does not shrink from
danger, hardship or bitter toil.*

Have we forgotten the sound of that President's voice? The sweet life of indifference and ease corrodes society. The creed of Machievelli must not assume any fancy popularity because it is totally opposed to the truth and to real success in life.

Many people will tell you that they desire to succeed, but not so many are prepared to pay the price. It is true that success is not always possible because external factors such as poverty, ill health, and inability prevent even the most courageous and ambitious from reaching their goals. Yet, we dare not exaggerate these circumstances to excuse negligence and its resultant failure. In most instances where there's a will to succeed there is also a way. It is appalling to encounter people who have the dreams of a duke but no more determination than a duck.

Many business men and managers unanimously concur that the modern craze for leisure and luxury, for more pay and less work, has created a situation of indifference, inefficiency, and indolence. No man can succeed unless he strives to master the cardinal virtues of dedicated determination, sincerity, and professional proficiency. With the poet we therefore pray:

58

*God give us men, a time like this demands*
*strong minds, great hearts, true faith*
*and steady hands,*
*Men whom the lust of office does not kill,*
*Men whom the spoils of office cannot buy,*
*Men who possess opinions and a will,*
*Men who love honor, men who cannot lie.*

This being true of our secular goals, it is also true of our spiritual goals that lead to our eternal destiny. To the early Christians, Saint Paul wrote; "If an athlete is willing to deny himself many things in order to win a prize that will pass away, we, too, must deny ourselves many things to win eternal life." Consider the astronauts, they serve day and night to go to the moon. We too, must serve day and night if we hope to go to Heaven. On our journey to Heaven there can be no rest, there can be no compromise with Satan or sin.

History shows that the average life span of the world's great civilizations is no more than 200 years. It is noted that great empires progress from bondage to liberty, from liberty to license, from license to indifference, and from indifference back to bondage. Should we not be fearful that our own civilization having progressed from "The Big Stick" to "The Great Society" is now faced with the deplorable danger of being debased by the sweet life?

There is some good in everybody, yet nobody loves God so much that he cannot love Him more. In each of us there is room for improvement. If we have fallen away from God, we must return and re-dedicate our lives to Him. Returning to God may well demand sacrifice and self-denial, but the time has come to make a spiritual stand. Those who do not stand for God always fall for the snares of Satan. Jesus said to His Apostles, "The servant is not greater than the master." If Christ had to pay the last drop of His Precious Blood for the redemption of mankind, we must surely be prepared to pay in some measure for our own.

Three major forces threaten our eternal destiny. The first is the Devil. Sometimes it appears that we no longer believe in Satan. At least we think very little about him. It does not bother us that he is the author of evil and sin. The Scriptures warn us, "The Devil comes and takes away the Word of God, so that the people cannot be saved." Has the Devil come to take away our integrity, or our honesty, or our purity?

The second disaster is Pride. We are inclined to think that since we can control the temperature of our homes and harness our rivers, we no longer need God. To think that we can live without God is the essence of pride. How little do we think of God? How seldom do we ask Him to help us? How often do we ignore Him? Recall the last major decision of your life and see who received attention and consideration. Was it yourself, your spouse, or your children? What about God? Did you consider Him at all?

The third disaster which threatens our destiny is "fascination with the world about us." Man's need for success and security must be placed in proper perspective. The pursuit of personal ambition and financial success must not become the Golden Calf, which instead of a blessing brought only a curse. It is folly to rely on the passing pleasures of this world. It is bad when our young can boast that they have tasted liquor and license, sex and sin. Pleasure derived from an inordinate desire for material prosperity does not promote either holiness or happiness.

Solomon was a wise man until he began to rely on his amount of gold. Because "much wants more" he increased his flocks and herds. Even then he was not satisfied, so he demanded more wives and women. Last of all, he paid homage to the false gods of his prostitutes. The pleasures of life became so absolute an obsession that he committed adultery and idolatry. He had lost his respect for law.

Four thousand years ago Hammurabi, the King of Babylon, based the first recorded law on the principle of "preventing the strong from oppressing the weak." We are told that there is law in

Heaven, and we know from history that God gave ten laws to Moses on Mount Sinai. Students of law are familiar with the legal codes of philosophers who have significantly contributed to the legislations of civilizations. Experts find value and wisdom in studying the decrees of Caesar, Justinian, and Napoleon. In England the Magna Carta was issued almost 800 years ago during the dispute between King John and his barons. Every school boy has heard of the Declaration of Independence. Over the centuries the Church has collected and framed a vast code of Canon Law.

While it may be that different lands have different laws, there is no land without law. Every nation, every society, every tribe, every business, and every family must have laws to insure safety and to enable mankind to live in peace and equality as brothers. Experience forbids any man to take the law into his own hands. The two world wars of the present century remind us that if a man becomes a law unto himself only the fittest survive.

Law by itself is not sufficient to safeguard man. Our federal laws and state statutes have not stopped the hemorrhage of crime in our land. It is estimated by the *National Councils on Crime and Delinquency* that criminality may be taking as much as $40 billion in profits each year. According to some authorities, it has invaded many apparently legitimate businesses such as banking, real estate, and industry. This knowledge prompts the conclusion that while law is necessary, it is not sufficient to solve the many injustices of life.

In the past we have not found the perfect human law. In the future we must recognize that our legal system will require constant and consistent updating. We may expect no more from the legal profession or the Supreme Court than we deserve. Experience has clearly established that a nation's law is no better than the sense of values of its people.

In addition to law, mankind needs a spirit of simplicity rather than a desire for status or success. In former times, the average American collegian was noted for his ambition to succeed and his desire for a career that would provide security and luxurious

*A Nation's law is no better than the sense of values of its people*

living. Nowadays, many of our students do not reflect that image. They prefer a way of life that is born of simplicity and an interest in asceticism. Many modern students feel that the life of materialism and luxury has been tried and failed. Consequently they seek a new way of life, and a way of social behavior that rejects overemphasis on economic prosperity.

In revolt against structural society, the new American, regardless of his cultural tradition, feels that it is his role to create a new social order that will humanize this world of technology and machines. Having been bitterly disappointed and disenchanted with the life of comfort and affluence, there is a growing tendency to seek emancipation from the bondage and limitations imposed on man by his reliance on material wealth. It is significant that status in society is no longer the essential mark of respect. Many youth are demanding a new style of life that is independent of externals. They know that externals are not always the faculty of truth. Their idea is to live without the feeling that it is necessary to own a fancy home and lavish furniture in order to be happy. They ask for freedom to do what they believe is best, so that life for them will be worthwhile.

Youths' ascetical way to happiness does not concern itself with the medical predictions that the lifespan of man will be prolonged by another twenty years before the end of the century. The modern approach does not fear death or life hereafter, it fears only unhappiness in the world we now live in. The fallacy of this attitude is that it does not consider the future. It beholds only the present moment.

But in fairness, we must admit that the modern approach of many students does not suggest that reason and revelation are antithetical. It does not say that scientific progress has rendered religion irrelevant or unnecessary. The new way values highly the consolations of convential creeds, but it demands that religious leaders break the barriers that sometimes prevent them from reaching people who are in desperate need of being reached and touched by religion. One of the reasons why people sometimes

*Revolt against structural society*

refuse to come to church is not because they find the discipline of the church too severe or the teachings of the church too incredible but because they find the structure of the church unventilated and impenetrable. Religion must allow a new spirit of faith to blow through its structure and open its gates for all classes to enter. This sentiment was expressed by Christ when He told Nicodemus:

*God loved the world so much that he gave His only Son,*
*so that everyone who believes in Him may not be lost*
*but may have eternal life.*
*God sent His Son into the world not to condemn the*
*world, but so that through Him the world might be saved.*

When we recall the story of Christ's life most of us do so incompletely. We remember that Jesus was born of a virgin mother in Bethlehem. We have a vague notion that when He was in His late twenties He began a campaign to establish the Church. His enemies succeeded in persuading the Roman Governor, Pontius Pilate, to issue a warrant for His execution. He was crucified, and at this point of crucifixion we finish the story of His life and of our Redemption. Our Redemption was not completed on the Cross, and the life of Christ did not end there.

The Christ we worship is the risen Christ. He rose from the dead and is living now. For many years the Resurrection did not receive its proper significance in the history of our salvation. It was regarded as nothing more than a proof that Jesus is Divine, and that He has command over life and death. It is erroneous to identify the resurrection as a mere motive of credibility. We do not find Christ among the dead but among the living. It may be heroic to die for the faith, but it is more heroic to live for the faith. Therefore, the renewal of our faith will be accomplished only when we re-discover the true meaning of Christ's purpose in rising from the dead.

Bishop Hugh A. Donohoe of Stockton, California, wrote to his people:

*Surely we believe the fact of resurrection, but we dare not relate it too closely to the whole scheme of our life. We are willing to accept it as one of those truths that are best described in esoteric fashion as eschatological.*

*We are reluctant to face up to the resurrection as something decisive in our day to day living. Surely, if one who was close to us returned from the dead, we would heed his every word and follow to the letter his every directive.*

In the early days of the church, the Apostles were not content to sit in the upper room and think about their good fortune in being chosen to be the first Christians. Instead, they went out bringing the good news to their fellowman.

During the centuries since then, Christian men and women have not ceased to spread the faith. Neither has persecution from without nor heresy from within faltered the growth of Christianity. Today, as in former ages, the spread of the faith depends on the people who hold it in trust. It is our duty not only to keep the faith but also to share it with others. If we are really convinced, we can not be satisfied until we share our convictions.

When a crowd of people gather together in one place, it is easy to forget the identity of each individual and his precious value in the eyes of God. But if we take one man from the crowd and reflect on his history and destiny, then we can understand God's great plan and love for every person. Take an example. There is a man in the crowd whose name is Ken. The story of Ken has no beginning, simply because God existed before time began. From the very beginning Ken lived in the infinite mind of God, God created the universe and made man, but all the time Ken was before His mind.

Adam fell. Cain killed Abel. Saul slew his thousands and David slaughtered many more. History brought joy and sorrow, war and peace, architecture and literature, music and song, television and sputniks. While all this was taking shape, God nursed the idea of Ken. In the fullness of time, God Himself became man. He was born for Ken, lived for Ken and died for Ken. For Ken too, He rose from the dead. At last in cooperation with Ken's parents, God procreated the body of Ken and gave him an immortal soul. Ken belongs to God. He must live with God. He must find his Father.

Like Ken, you have history and destiny. Every man must seek his Father. Millions however, whose number is known only to God, are going the wrong way. Like sheep without a shepherd, they are waiting for some good shepherd to show them the right way. How many of these un-enlightened souls do you meet in a given day? How many disillusioned people do you touch in the course of life? There is much joy and happiness that you can give to others if you are willing to share your faith. Jesus likened the faith to a lamp, but He added:

*A lamp is not lit to be put under a bushel but on a lamp-stand so that men can see the light. You are the light of the world, let your light shine before men.*

There will always be a great multitude of people in this world for whom only your lamp will light the way of salvation. Men are not always convinced and converted by what they read and hear, but by what they see through the light of your life. In silent awe men recognize that the ineffable virtues of Faith, Hope, and Love make us all brothers in Christ.

As brothers of Christ we are summoned to seek and manifest the real truth. We dare not reduce His teachings to a matter of private speculation or exploit it to serve the personal fantasy of any individual. Divine Providence has decreed that our efforts to spread the faith must at all times be expedited in union with Christ. Only in union with Him can our efforts contribute to the building up of His Mystical Body which is the Church.

No man can be a successful witness to Christ unless he keeps in his heart a genuine devotion to the Church and a special affection and concern for its world-wide extensions. Christ captured the hearts of men by being "all things to all men." He mourned with those who had lost a friend. He lived with those who were poor. He dined with the rich, and with the Doctors of the Law He held conferences. We cannot be His disciples unless we identify ourselves with those whom we propose to convert. Respect for the opinions of others will keep open the channels of communication with them. By normal conversation and friendship it is possible to discern the weaknesses of associates. By knowing what is weak we can take measures to make it strong. By having love in our hearts, we can share with others the "wonderful things God has in store for those who love Him."

If the heart is hard like a stone, change it into a heart of love where the seed of faith will bloom and grow. By working now to spread the Faith, we pay in advance the price of destiny.

*All things to all men*

# Tomorrow Will Be Beautiful

Looking back on 1968 A.D. one almost shudders at the sequence of events. The world was shocked as eight million Ibo warriors slowly starved in the civil war between Nigeria and secessionist Biafra. North Korea took the USS PUEBLO on the high seas. The largest earthquake in the history of Iran killed 20,000 people and left 100,000 without homes. In Czechoslovakia 200,000 Russian and Warsaw Pact soldiers invaded the land to curtail the reforms of Premier Dubcek's Government. Riots in Mexico City threatened the Olympic Games and anti-draft demonstrators disrupted the proceedings at the Democratic Party Convention in Chicago. The Poor built Resurrection City, and the world mourned the tragic killing of Martin L. King and Robert F. Kennedy.

The record is sad but it is not complete. In the same year we all shared the joy of Dr. Christian Bernard, who performed the world's first successful transplant of a human heart. In Rome the leader of Christendom proclaimed the Credo of the People of God. At the instigation of President Lyndon B. Johnson the Vietnam Peace Conference began in Paris. On Christmas Eve three Americans orbited round the moon and from their lunar module reminded us that "In the beginning God created the heavens and the earth."

From the first moment of creation the world has not ceased its motion. So, too, mankind is in motion, and he forever vibrates with happiness and hunger, loneliness and love. These vibrations of man emanate from people who share with each other their convictions and desires. People vibrate at varied frequencies because the French are not like the Americans, and the English are different from the people of Japan. Diversity gives meaning to life.

In his infinite wisdom God created all men equal and made each man unique. When God made you, it was not His intention that you should spend your days imitating the lives of others.

*"In the beginning God created the heavens and the earth"*

In the eyes of God each person is someone special. Somebody once told me that everyone has a double. That is not true because men are like a kaleidoscope in which the same design is never repeated.

Those who seek to imitate the lives of great men such as Lincoln or Churchill are doomed to failure. The reason is strictly theological. We know that God is building up a wonderful unity from the whole universe of men. This unity we call The Mystical Body of Christ. Each person in that Body is absolutely unique. Each of us has been deliberately "chosen in Christ from all eternity." In the mind of God each man has a unique personality. It follows then that each man can only be what God wants him to be. If a man is true to himself, that is, true to God's idea of him, he will be successful in fulfilling his special role which The Creator has reserved for him in this world. This is the basic truth of God's word to Israel, "I have loved you with an everlasting love, so I am constant in my affection for you."

Let us suppose that by dint of great determination you endeavored to model yourself like unto Abraham Lincoln. It seems to me that God would say, "I wanted Abraham Lincoln; that is why I created him; but I also wanted you. I made you, and now I have only a caricature of you."

It is vitally important that each man strive to be his true self. No man is his true self starting out in life. There are layers of falsehood in every man. The truth of each man's personality is centered on God and on loving Him. In practice, however, we are too often self-centered and self-loving. In the Christian life the whole point of prayer and penance and instruction is to eliminate the falsity and release and reveal the true personality. Many people have twisted themselves out of recognition by not being their true selves.

Yet there is one whom we may unconditionally imitate. That one is Christ. He is the true Word, now made flesh, in whom each of us was chosen before time began. Being the fullness of truth, He contains the truth of all personalities. He is the mystery behind

73

*In the eyes of God each person is someone special*

every good deed that you perform.

If you attempt to explain fully why you do good or how you do it, you will find yourself delving deeply into the mystery of the Blessed Trinity. Even the smallest good act has been eternally prepared by God, and with great love. The grace that moves us to help a friend has been won for us on the heights of Calvary. The power of the devil who seeks the corruption of man has already been overpowered by the victory of the Cross. Yet it is erroneous to propose that the triumph of Calvary assures the Christianization of man. The Christianization of any man depends on his willingness to use his natural faculties in conjunction with the supernatural and gracious help of Christ.

Let us not underestimate the native skills of human nature. The talents that God has given us surpass the greatest instrumentalities of our own making. Were I a millionaire and able to afford the most expensive lens in all the world, that lens, valuable as it may be, could not give me the joy that is mine when I open my eyes and see a thing of beauty — a rose or a willow tree or a trustful smile. Or if I were an engineer and able to produce the most sensitive tape recorder, that receiver would not give me the satisfaction I experience when I listen with my own ear to a merry little wren filling the air with melody and song.

The nature of man is human, and that is why he must use his natural talents if he wishes to Christianize his life. Have you ever thought of the glory you give to God or of the service you give to another man when you use your natural talents in the best possible way? You seek happiness, but you will find it only on that night when you can say, "This day I used all my faculties and all my talents to the best of my ability."

Every word, every motion, every thought that you have must be directed toward the emancipation of your creative genius and skills. You do not have to be an ordinary man—it is your privilege to be a great man. But in order to accomplish anything, in order to leave something to posterity, in order to promote understanding and good will, you must not forever bemoan the times or

*Or a trustful smile*

seek refuge in elusive unanimity or spend your days waiting for directives. You must act now! You must dedicate your time and your energy and your personality to the service of one another.

On this day you must decide what cause you will serve, what course you will follow. Those who live from day to day, from week to month, from month to year leave nothing to the world but the memory of their frustrations and stupidities. You must reach your decision now. Decide now how you can illuminate the world. Decide now how you can utilize every gift that you have, and having made your decision, let no man daunt your efforts.

Work at your goal from dawn 'til dark, and when the night comes, retire early to renew and refresh yourself for the "great, big, beautiful tomorrow." It is sad, it is bad, to see the lack of order, the lack of cleanliness, the lack of moral strength that follows him who begins his day with the disadvantage of a late rising. You must rise early to read, to think, to plan, to pray, and to work. It is only when we learn to discipline ourselves and use our talents that we can truthfully say "the confusion of the world is not a ruling law." On the contrary, the Law of Christ is mankind's guiding star. There once were three wise men who followed that star and found Christ. Those of us who believe in Christ are summoned now to follow that star, so that we, too, will find Christ.

In resounding tones the noted French singer, Maurice Chevalier, has sung for us the good news:

*There's a great, big, beautiful tomorrow,*
*Shining at the end of every day.*
*There's a great, big, beautiful tomorrow,*
*And tomorrow's just a brink away.*
*Man has a dream and that's the start.*
*He follows his dream with mind and heart.*
*And when it becomes a reality,*
*It's a dream come true for you and me.*
*So there's a great, big, beautiful tomorrow,*
*Shining at the end of every day.*
*There's a great, big, beautiful tomorrow;*
*Just a brink away.*

The problems facing the world are no greater than ourselves. If we are willing, we shall overcome our problems, great and small. We shall dry our tears; we shall forget our fears if we believe that tomorrow will be beautiful.

*"Great, big, beautiful tomorrow"*

# Signs of Gladness

We who live in California live close to wineries. The Golden West has many orchards and well-tended vineyards. Wine to suit every taste and type is easily available. And yet it is a special art to make good wine. It requires much patience and skill to season and prepare the fruit of the vine. Every hand must be clean, every grape must be good, every barrel must be fresh, and the fermentation leisurely and slow. Albeit the grapes must be crushed, there is joy, too, in the making of wine because of the happiness it will bring and the hospitality it affords when a friend drops by. The world over, we recognize in the glass of wine the sign of welcome and respect. It is a gleam of gladness. It is a medium of communication between men, be they friends or acquaintances.

For centuries, men of learning have sought the best medium of communication. That is something we hardly ever think of. Every day we depend on signs and use them to communicate with the people who live in our house, or share in our work, or attend the same restaurant for lunch. For example, in youthful romance there is a time when love is so profound that those in love feel desperately incapable of adequately expressing their love. The external expression of one's inmost sentiment is not possible. We may, however, circumvent the impossibility by giving a gift as a dear token or sign of our heartfelt thoughts. The monetary or material value of the gift is not important. What really matters is what the gift stands for, and how it is received by the one who is loved. Objectively considered, a school ring is of little value, but it has a deep meaning and high beauty when it is meant to say, "You are someone very special; you are my only friend."

"Do not consider," wrote Thoman a 'Kempis, "the gift of the lover, but only the love of the giver." Many times and in many ways we use signs to relate our feelings and convictions to other people. The fundamental medium of human communication is a sign of one kind or another.

*"You are someone very special; you are my only friend"*

Speech is a sign of communication. So, too, is touch. What sound or words of love can surpass the intimacy of a single kiss? More than half of Christ's miracles were effected by the sense of touch. Every priest who has whispered the act of contrition into the ear of a dying man knows that there is gratitude in the slight pressure he feels on his hand. Every student of medicine knows that he cannot heal the sick man until he is brave enough to touch him. The ordination of a priest is complete only when the bishop touches the head of the young man.

Emotion too is a sign of communication. The great Lebanese philosopher, Kahlil Gibran, believed that emotion is a fundamental medium of communication. It is recorded by Saint John that when Lazarus died "Jesus wept." As he did so, the Jews who watched Him said one to the other, "See how much He loved him." Traditionally, we have relegated our emotions to a minor role in our study of man. We have been unmindful of the fact that our emotions have an impact on every human act, and that is why emotion has been doctored and debased by human hands. One may endeavor to conceal and control his emotions, but the moment his soul is pre-occupied by joy or grief, his emotions become a sign of communication. No man can prevent others from interpreting his emotions for they are signs of communication. This is why many philosophers teach their students that man is known not by his actions but by his reactions.

Sound, touch, emotion, the barber's red and white pole, the lines on the freeway, are all signs of communication. We need these signs, and we react to them every day. At times it may be that the channels of communication get tied up, but we must have signs to communicate with other men. This being the case, it should not be too difficult to understand that if a man needs signs to communicate with another man, he also needs signs to communicate with God.

We need signs about God, for as John the Baptist put it, "There is one in the midst of you whom you do not know." It would be unwise to suggest that going to Church on Sundays is the absolute

*Man needs signs to communicate with God*

essence of true Christianity. Numerical success is no norm of religion, and the records of deeds well done or of goals accomplished do not assure salvation. Yet the fact that less than fifty percent of adult Americans attend weekly services is an indication that the words of John the Baptist are still relevant. Only sixty-six percent of adult Catholics go to Sunday Mass, and the typical attendance of other denominations at Sunday worship is less than forty percent. "There is one in the midst of us whom we do not know," and so we must learn again the signs of God.

Jesus instituted seven signs to lead us to God. These signs we call Sacraments. A Sacrament may be defined as a sign instituted by Christ so that man can communicate with God. By using these signs we can understand that God is not a statue made of wood or stone, but a living Father whose love for each person is so intense that it is meant to draw forth a tremendous response of love and trust in return. God is not a remote being who is in constant competition with us. He is a real person who seeks to communicate with us through signs such as bread and wine; signs we can understand as readily as we understand the meaning of flowers or of a wedding band.

Matrimony is the sign of Christian love. Anointing of the sick is a sign that suffering need not be in vain. Holy Orders is the sign of "Another Christ." Holy Communion is the sign of God's love for man. Confession is the sign of repentance and forgiveness. Confirmation is the sign of Christian witness. Baptism is the sign of Christian initiation.

There are different kinds of signs. Some signs signify something as a neon light signifies the location of a store. Other signs contain what they signify. A flower is a sign that signifies scent and also contains the ingredients of perfume. So too, the sacraments are signs that signify Christ and also contain Christ.

The use of these sacramental signs is the most direct medium we have to communicate with God. They are our points of contact with Him. They unite us to Him which is the essential prerequisite of being a Christian. "A branch cannot bear fruit unless it is united to the vine," and a man cannot be a Christian unless he is united to Christ. "Without me," says Christ, "you can do nothing." He alone is the source of Christian thought, emotion, and action. He alone is "the way, the truth, and the life." The fundamental reason for the existence of the church is that she would confect the sacraments and administer them to the people, so that the people can communicate with God and unite themselves to Him.

The grace of God that is received through these signs is best invested in every dimension of daily life, for the actual living according to these signs in turn generates grace, and has a value of its own that is recognized in heaven.

Living the Christian life is not easy. When Christ was still an infant, his mother, Mary, took him to the temple. While they were there, she met an old man named Simeon. He took the child in his arms and spoke in prophecy saying, "Behold, this child is destined for the fall and for the rise of many in Israel, and for a sign of contradication." The subsequent years of Christ's life proved the truth of that prophecy. He told His disciples to take up their cross, and he gave them the supreme example when He was literally nailed to the cross. Ever since that crucifixion, the crucifix has been loved and venerated by Christians.

During the first decade of the third century, the city of Rome was captured by a young soldier called Constantine. His father and mother were both pagans who gave worship to the sun. Constantine was indifferent to religion as a spiritual heritage, but his soldier's subtlety and acumen warned him that a unifying bond was necessary to keep together the army which he had mustered from a league of nations and a variety of cultures. For this reason he obliged his men to be Christians. For himself, however, he remained an atheist until the battle of the Milvian Bridge. On the night before that battle, while resting a few miles outside Rome, he had a dream in which he was told to engrave on the shields of his soldiers the Sign of the Cross before entering the next day's battle. It was done. Constantine won the day and took Rome with the cry of the Christians, "In hoc signo vinces"—by this sign you will conquer.

The Sign of the Cross is not easily discovered. It is a hidden treasure. It is a pearl of great price, not a common commodity available on the market. Yet it is our task to find that sign and bring it to those who have not yet discovered it. It is our role to bring that sign to the walk-ups and to the hippies in San Francisco's Golden Gate Park and New York's Greenwich Village. We've got to carry that sign to the campuses of our universities and to our senators in their red leather chairs. We must build that sign in our prisons and skid-rows. We must erect that sign in the barracks of our soldiers and in the mansions of Beverly Hills.

The Cross is the sign of Christ who said to those who loved Him, "If you wish to be my disciples, take up your cross every day and come follow me." To be a Christian is to be a Sign of God. The Father is Life. The Word of God is Truth. The Spirit of God is Love. The Christian is the sign of all three — life, truth, and love.

Every minute ninety babies are born on this planet, but 10,000 people die each day of malnutrition. There are approximately 980 million children in the world, but 600 million of them have not the basic dignities of humanity. That is a problem we shall not solve by preventing life but only by sharing the Christian Life. There is nothing more precious than being a Christian. If we lose our Christianity, we lose all. "What does it profit a man if he gain the whole world and suffer the loss of his soul?"

The vocation to be a Christian does not come from man but from God. God may choose to call you through a friend, that is why you must stay in a state of alert abandonment to His will, watching always for the signs of His call, doing what you can to further it, being ready someday to embrace it when it comes, knowing all the time that He has something better in store for you than your wildest dreams. It is this state of dependence in darkness that gives thrill to life, makes it exciting, makes it Christian.

The world in which we live is confused about many things. A multitude of value systems devour the very core of society. Our toleration of naturalism and our inclination toward humanism and technological scientism have set in motion a malicious campaign to destroy religion. Have you not heard it said that Christianity is an obsolete myth that is rapidly disintegrating into a series of pious platitudes that have no place in our modern society? By intimidating one-half of our people and confusing the other, these sinister attacks have undermined our trust in Christ.

The great weapon of the criminal is the trembling timidity of the law-abiding citizen. The modern Christian must not be afraid to lead warlike attacks on all that is ignoble and rotten in his environment. We need more than happy Christians with nun-smile teeth. Let us arise from the slumber of indifference and ease. Let us attack the whole sordid hypocrisy of those who attend church on Sunday and remain indifferent to the moral issues that confront every family of society every day of the week. It is not enough to love what is good. We are also called to hate what is evil, and in hating it, to do our utmost to destroy it.

In destroying the wickedness of our surroundings, we are summoned not to engage in pagan brutality or violence, but to an intelligent and mature undertaking of responsibility. The reform this world urgently needs is one that leads to the perfection of mankind, not by revolution but by evolution. Only with courage and innovating transformations can we channel Christianity into the service of all men without creating new injustices or provoking new wars.

We might describe the state as an institution that is called by God to safeguard man's body. The church is divinely established to protect and promote the well-being of man's soul. Government officials will seek to improve a man by improving his environment, but it is not sufficient to improve the house in which a man lives. It is more beneficial to improve the man who lives in a house.

The role of the church begins where that of the state ends. It is the church's duty to teach those who live in ghettos and slums to understand that they have a responsibility to help themselves. It would not cost too much to clean the slums if each man would learn to fix his own house, wash his own window, and paint his own door. This area of the Christian Apostolate calls for our immediate attention. Every Christian should be willing and proud to help the man who is sick or unable to provide for himself. That does not mean that the good man who works hard should be obliged to neglect his own immediate needs in order to provide for those who are able but unwilling to provide for themselves.

Christianity does not claim to have solutions for every problem or resources to terminate every conflict. Christianity is a challenge facing each man to search for an understanding of the complex process of man's growth, physically and psychologically, socially and spiritually. Christianity does not seek a way out that ignores our problems but a way forward, to our final destiny.

The value system which we inherit from the life and teaching of Christ is still relevant, but is fruitful only when each person is willing to receive the signs of faith and act accordingly. It is not enough to know the law of Christ; we must translate that law into every thought and every act of every day. Neither are isolated gestures of good-will or holiness any criterion of Christianity. What Christ expects of his followers is a total style of living that results from a constant response and reaction to His philosophy.

In every age, the church has had her saints and scholars. All over the world she has sent her missionaries and martyrs to show mankind some signs about God. Every generation of Christians for two thousand years has faced that challenge and has brought new life to men. Yet we cannot afford to rest on the honors of the past, for Christianity is not an ornament of history. It is rather a living and dynamic way of life that matures with the people who, in keeping it themselves, simultaneously share it with others.

Christians are the chosen people of God. They are sons of God the Father, and signs of God the Son. They have a special and most holy role in their duty to keep Christianity alive and to spread it from their own homes, even to the ends of the earth. In the fulfillment of that sacred task there is the principle of loyalty to the church. In our presentation of the Christian philosophy we dare not depart from the authority of the church. Those who neglect the authorized testimony of Christ confuse the people and destroy the unity of the human family. In his first Epistle to the Corinthians the Apostle Paul wrote this heartfelt plea:

*I appeal to you, my brothers, in the name of Our Lord, Jesus Christ, that all of you agree and that there be no dissensions among you, but that you be united in the same mind and the same judgment.*

That is a message we cannot disregard. It does not submerge the voice of individual conscience. It asks only that the individual conscience be formed and also informed. Christianity does not exclude new ideas or turbulent spirits, but it seeks to form them according to the mind of Christ.

At the Last Supper, Jesus took a goblet of wine and having blessed it He gave it to His disciples and said:

*This is the cup of my Blood,*
*The Blood of the new and everlasting covenant—*
*The mystery of Faith.*
*This Blood is to be shed for you and for all men*
*So that sins may be forgiven.*

Although the grapes must be crushed there is joy in the making of wine. So, too, there is joy in being a Christian because the cup of Christ's Blood is a sign of salvation for all men. That sign is truly something special. Do not clasp it so close that you crush its spirit,

*Grapes must be crushed — there is joy in making the wine*

or so tight that you break its ambition and daring.

Those who have the Spirit of Christ are free. Those who bear the sign of Christ are wild. They cannot be tamed completely. Leave them with Christ, for they are the signs of gladness.

# The Destiny

All over the world, young men of vision and old men of dreams speak to us of the future as the ancient prophets spoke of the past. The renowned scholar and scientist, Jacques Ellul, predicts in his book THE TECHNOLOGICAL SOCIETY, that startling changes in Religion and Social Behaviors will already be in effect by the end of the century. The population of the world will probably jump from the present 3.5 billion persons to 7 billion.

Before continuing to speculate on the future state of the Union, it is imperative to make some reasonable assumptions even though all assumptions contain uncertainties and risks.

Unless some unforeseen calamity interrupts our economic growth, we can expect an annual average increase of two and one-half percent in the cost of living which indicates that our consumer spending will reach a peak of more than one trillion dollars by 1980. The warning of Mark Twain, that man is the only animal that deliberately seeks to annihilate his own kind, is a sign that the cost of military measures will remain tremendously high. Our building of houses will zoom to an average of two million a year for the next decade. This increase in housing will necessitate a proportionate increase in the production of everything that goes into house construction, fixtures and furnishings. Automobile manufacturers expect the increase in population to result in an annual average purchase of fifteen million autos during the 1970's.

In the field of Education it is predicted that the difficult process of study will not be necessary. Knowledge, we are told, will be stored in "electronic banks." Information on any subject may be obtained from electronic machines that will impart the required knowledge directly to the brain. But Education will endure, for the mind of man must mature.

In fact, if present trends continue, it is estimated that overall educational costs will increase by forty percent during the next ten years. The projected enrollment for the school-year, 1977-

1978, approximates sixty three million students in the United States at a cost of seventy-six billion dollars. The greatest enrollment increase will be at the college and the high school level because the majority of students who will be in the upper grade bracket during the latter part of the next decade were born during high birth-rate years. As a result higher education spending will probably rise sixty percent.

Young people in the future will represent not merely a group of great numerical magnitude, but they will also constitute an independent reality within our society. The culture and social changes that are forever influencing the world will affect the majority of students and not just a minority of colored radicals or white militants.

Formerly, the adult establishment directed our youth through structured institutions such as the family, places of work, and centers of learning.

Nowadays, our young people make up a new social order that has its own peculiar value-system. Consequently, if we hope to direct and give momentum to this new order, we must search for new responsibilities and new roles in the American community.

It is easy in modern and popular jargon to dismiss the radical student unrest that is extending itself from universities to high schools as a negative force designed only to foster anarchy and disorder. While it is too near events to judge with a proper perspective the final outcome of student activism, we must re-assess at this point the duty of educators to take the initiative in co-ordinating student behavior with solid democratic principles. To do less will result in repressive precautions that will intensify the issue. Campus activism, if given proper leadership, will instill in our students a deeper awareness of the social problems that face the nation. Students must appreciate that they have a duty to involve themselves in seeking solutions.

The campus reform should not terminate in chaos, for it was originally intended to re-define our sense of values in a manner that would meet the needs of society now and in the future without dishonoring our heritage. Ultimately, someone will have to decide whether activism will be crushed by force or whether it will be used as a platform where curriculum improvement and the relationship between freedom and responsibility can be re-evaluated and re-defined.

Since half of our population is under twenty-five, one out of every three Americans will be in school within another few years. To provide adequately for this need, it is predicted that educators will launch a brilliant campaign of floating schools where students of art will attend the Museum of Art, and the students of english will occupy the benches in our Free Public Libraries. Students of journalism will be apprenticed to the local newspaper, and so on. In this way educators will share with the local community the responsibility of providing education for those who are young.

But society will not be content to educate only those who are young. Special emphasis will be placed on adult education, for that is a function of Church and Civic obligation that is beginning to awaken from a slumber of deplorable longevity. Because society seems to be leisure-pleasure oriented, it will not be long until men will be off work three days per week and enjoy three months vacation per year. Thus, we should have the time and the opportunity to reach and educate the adult world.

The future of family-life is a matter of speculation. The value of genetically devising human offspring for particular professions and places is not clearly understood. Likewise, the question of parthenogenesis and the ability of medical science to predetermine the sex of children by dis-joining the androsperm, that produces boys, from the gynosperm, that produces girls remain unsettled. But whathever the outcome of these speculations it is salutary to remember that the function of sex is procreation and mutual solace within marriage and not a source of recreation to be used at will.

The color problem will be with us in the years that lie ahead. There will never be a color-blind city as long as one particular group monopolizes certain occupations or controls the status of certain areas. For the same reason the ghettos of our time will not easily die. It is noted that the different classes of men are not evenly distributed throughout our society. A ghetto is not a slum. A slum is known by the fact that its people are poor. A ghetto is known by the fact that its residents hold the same values, possess the same inclinations, and share the same ambitions. Consequently, we must work toward the material and spiritual enrichment of our less fortunate brothers.

Vocations to the ministry will increase and find a new meaning and relevance in the mystery and confusion of society. So, too, in the midst of all the motion and action men will find time to pray. "Action to the productive has need of contemplation." In the future new orders of contemplatives will flourish and discover for us the true value of the new dimension of Christian thought and philosophy.

Religion is not and never has been a completed castle. It is forever in the process of being built. Its bulwarks are the people, its cornerstone is God. Therefore, we must believe in God, and trust in Him, knowing that He makes no mistakes. He is the Divine Potter who skillfully moulds the fragile clay of which we are made. He is the Master Craftsman, and we are apprentices whom He has chosen to stand and serve.

I once heard of an Oriental Monarch who asked his wise men for a sentence that would always be true; and they presented him with the words, "This too shall pass away." For us who live in the 20th century these words at first sight appear to be true. Everything nowadays is shortlived. If you buy a hat or gown this fall, it is very likely that the fashions will have changed so much by next year that you will will have to buy again. And likewise in other walks of life—new fashions, styles, and ideas—all tend to hasten the exit of what is old, to make way for what is new.

But if we pause and consider the words of the wise men, we see that they are not strictly true because we believe in a life to come—in a life that will not pass away—one which will never end. We believe in God, who always was and always will be, and we believe it is our duty to give Him due honor and worship. That is our destiny; to love God and to live with God forever.

On July 4, 1776, our fathers assembled in Congress and adopted the Declaration of Independence. The last words of the Declaration read:

> *And for the support of this Declaration, with a firm reliance on the protection of Divine Providence we mutually pledge to each other, our lives, our fortunes, and our sacred honor.*

In 1976 we will commemorate the second centenary of the Declaration of Independence. We will undoubtedly recall that the Declaration stands before the world as the symbol of truth and liberty. It has given to our people the knowledge—

> *That all men are created equal, that they are endowed by their creator with certain inalienable rights, that among these are Life, Liberty and the Pursuit of Happiness.*

The Declaration is indeed the generous giver of knowledge, religious, scientific, and artistic. It has given to life religion, recreation, and refinement. It has advanced both the cultural and industrial arts. Our pride in that Declaration is a common bond that inspires us to maintain it and to look to the future with the fullest confidence. We are proud and happy as the second centenary of its adoption draws near, and the reflection of that pride and happiness is a blessing on us all.

As we prepare to celebrate the occasion in 1976, let us be mindful that our nation has defied for centuries the blandishments and bribes of the godless and the heretical. And so it is altogether fitting that we in our time examine ourselves with soul-searching zeal.

We note that in 1954, Congress decreed that the words "Under God" be returned to the Pledge of Allegiance to the flag of the United States. The coins of our money bear the inscription "In God We Trust." Compared to other Nations there is a high degree of religiosity in our land. On a typical Sunday fifty million Americans attend church services.

Dr. George H. Gallup, Jr., President of the American Institute of Public Opinion, reported in December 1968 that ninety-eight percent of the Americans surveyed by his office indicated that they believe in God. There is pride in that, and yet we know that "As the body without the Spirit is dead, so also faith without good works is dead."

Therefore, fully conscious of our many faults, we place ourselves and our ideals under the protection of God. His blessing we invoke. It is our prayer that we will not dishonor Him by inhumanity, immorality, or indifference. We pledge to respect the rights of all men and to restore consolation and compassion in this age of computers and cybernetics.

I once had the occasion to perform the burial service of an old violinist who was found frozen to death in the snow. Speaking as the beneficiary of this man, I acknowledge my debt to him, for it seems to me that he has shown us how to achieve the destiny. In my experience I do not recall so strongly the impact of any other funeral service upon me, at least in a form which has so long endured in my memory or conscience. Allow me to tell you the story of this violinist in these words.

Feeble and frail he shivered there
Lonely and poor and old.
The snow dank on his thin grey hair
His cheeks were blue with cold.

Wistfully gazed through the window bright
At the cozy warmth within;
Whispered a prayer on that winter night
They would let a beggar man in.

Slowly he drew from beneath his coat
A violin, mellow and old.
Raised his bow with shivering hand
And fingers numb with cold.

Dear God, he prayed, let me play once more
Of childhood's scenes so fair,
Of river and valley, lake and moor,
Of the joys of yesteryear.

He played of America, land of dreams;
Of beauty everywhere.
Of moonbeams dancing on silvan streams
Of glens and mountains there.

Forgotten the biting winter cold,
Forgotten the moaning storm;
But a garden fair with roses there,
And birdies thrilling song.

And lo, he hears the Angel call
"Come, clean of heart," he said.
"We need another in choirs above."
To the heavenly home he led.

They found him next morn in the frozen snow,
Ragged and old and dead.
Just a shrug as they pushed aside,
"A violinist beggar" they said.

But in the heavenly choirs that day
Was a new and jubilant chord;
For in heaven also do violins play,
And the player was now with the Lord.

If the violinist attained the destiny, it is our turn to seek it now.

It is true that we live in times of rapid social and economic change. In former times similar circumstances led man to a rationalization that caused him to lose many sacred values. Let us be careful then, lest the innovations of our day lead to the desacramentalization of our lives. The fact that we live in a world of change is a challenge to every man because each of us must decide what to abandon and what to accept. Futuriology alerts us to the pressures that change imposes on man and on his environment. It warns us that sociology and theology must not be separated, for man must not be separated from God. Let us not forget that only Christ could say, "Behold, I make all things new."

Dream of Destiny when in turmoil and tears, for there is serenity in the silence of dreams. Speak the truth calmly and clearly for the truth shall set you free. Listen quietly to all men, even the unlettered and unwise; they, too, have a dream and a destiny.

Do not identify yourself with offensive persons, for they will infect the peace of your soul. If you imitate others you may become sad because God wants you to be yourself. Likewise, if you envy others you will surely twist yourself out of recognition.

Be cautious in the face of danger but do not underestimate the value of your own talents. They are more wonderful than the greatest instrumentalities of technology.

Be honest with yourself. Cherish with care the precious pearl of love, for in the face of all adversity it will give tranquility and happiness.

Accept with understanding the wisdom of experience but add to it the enthusiasm of youth.

Prepare your soul for sudden sadness, but do not indulge in loneliness for there will always be a beautiful tomorrow. You are a child of the God and it is your right to call Him "Father." He has a plan for you that is greater than your wildest dreams. Whether you understand it or not, someday, He will unfold it before your eyes. If you love God, your dreams, however incomprehensible or shattered they may be, will lead you to your Destiny.

Like men who have reached the hilltop, we look up at the Great Mountain that stands in the distant mist and summons us to climb. We must not fear to go up there where the air is crisp and cool, where the mind is clear and calm, where the eye can see what it never saw, where the intellect can capture thoughts that never were and conceive the glory of Eternal Life and receive it abundantly.

Eternal Life ought to be the dream of every man. In any event it is the destiny of us all.

102